TSS WHITEBOARD SELLING

FOREWORD

In my role as a sales leader for IBM's Technology Support Services, I was looking for a better method to explain and provide consultancy to our customers on how to optimize their Information Technology infrastructure support so they can profit from higher availability and lower cost. In 2011 I came across the IBM Whiteboard Selling Method, which was a stark departure from our past methods focused on sales techniques.

With a bit of research we deployed this consulting methodology on our TSS Academy platform and provided this insightful tool for free to anyone interested in understanding their customers better. In 2012, in snow covered Austria, we put the theory into practice in the first TSS Champion Education focused on a case study that evolved over the three days of the workshop.

Teaching the methodology on several occasions myself, I got more deeply immersed and started to understand the finer aspects of how to optimize support. With the help of my former manager and mentor Neil Thubron, the psychological background was made transparent and we generalized the concept to be used in any situation.

The principles are applicable to any consulting situation, and today I use the methodology whenever I need to explore and work with other people to find optimal solutions with better outcomes.

I have witnessed people using the Whiteboard Selling Method to transform their approach to customers, increase their revenue significantly and change the course of their career in a very positive way. Deploying the methodology in Europe, we kept our revenue growing in a declining market and are working to roll it out on a global scale to Business Partners worldwide.

Having reaped the benefits myself, I encourage you to read and re-read the book, implement what you feel comfortable with and come back for more. I am convinced that you will feel the benefits of collaborating with your customers and grow your business - like others did before you!

Meggen, January 2018, Beat Erb

INTRODUCTION: WHY WHITEBOARD SELLING

'You never lose a deal on price. You only ever lose on not selling enough value.' – Mladen Kresic

This quote from Mladen Kresic neatly summarises and introduces our philosophy behind the whiteboard methodology and strategy: that if enough value can be demonstrated to a client, price becomes significantly less important for them and the likelihood of making a sale goes up dramatically.

I have been using and teaching the whiteboard tool for over ten years, in TSS and in other divisions at IBM. Having worked as a salesperson, a sales manager and more recently as director of sales across Europe, I have seen this technique in action and the results that it can achieve. I have employed the method in the boardroom at Nestlé, at Barclays Bank and countless other client situations, big and small, with great success. In short, it works!

The central aim of the whiteboard methodology is to identify what is really important to the client, what they truly value from a business and personal perspective, and to then build up the value of your service by linking your solution to exactly what they are looking for. If we imagine that a transaction is a set of scales, on the one side you have the price of your service, and on the other side you have the value that it will deliver. We want our clients to be focusing their attention on the latter part of the scales, and the greater the value the easier this becomes. By associating the value of your service with their needs and their reasons for wanting to buy, the price will always be less of an issue.

Different types of value

There are different kinds of values that we can develop when working through the whiteboard with a client. We can divide these roughly into 'left brain' and 'right brain' values, i.e. logical and emotional. The logical side is the facts and figures that make up and back up your solution: the business case and pound note values. The emotional side, on the other hand, addresses the personal aspects of why a client is trying to achieve their goal. What is driving them, what excites them.

While it is certainly important to address both of these kinds of values – logical and emotional – we have found that clients make decisions based much more on their emotions than on logic. Working on the emotional side will help to reinforce the logical side and make it seem more appealing. Having all the facts and figures in place gives the client permission to make their decision based on their emotions.

This is not a new idea. All the way back in Ancient Greece Aristotle wrote about the persuasive power of leaders who focused on 'pathos' (emotional values) in their speeches over 'logos' (logical ones). He found that the most persuasive speeches had 65% pathos - words, tone, content - 25% Lagos and 10% Ethos (ethics).

The purpose, then, of the whiteboard selling methodology is to uncover the client's values, both business and personal, to uncover their real drivers, the real reasons they are aiming for their goal, and to ensure that your solution is aligned with those reasons and those values.

Why whiteboard over other sales techniques

There are many different sales techniques out there, many of them touted by very successful salespeople, so why did we choose whiteboard for TSS?

First of all, it focuses on the individual client before anything else. You don't start talking about your service or the features and benefits of your solution until you understand how those features and benefits could really add value to their business. It's very easy for salesmen to jump straight from, 'What do you need, Mr Customer?' to 'Well, here's something that will fix that for you,' rather than going a little bit deeper. The whiteboard technique asks more questions. It goes a couple of layers down into the client's real business reasons and real personal reasons for wanting to buy.

Second, it's got a very logical and simple design, which has been carefully created so that it flows in the way the brain thinks and will make sense to a client quickly and easily. Starting with the goal in the centre you take them – moving from left to right on the board – away from their challenges and towards your solution (we'll be looking in more detail at the structure of the whiteboard throughout the course of the book).

Finally, the whiteboard is very visually impactful. A picture paints a thousand words, as the saying goes, and so by using the whiteboard with its carefully design colours and layout we can help the client visualise the journey they're going to go on with you.

One point to note here is that whiteboard selling doesn't have to be done on an actual whiteboard. It can be in a notebook, on a flipchart, on a napkin in a restaurant – I've even coached people using the whiteboard methodology by sitting next to them and writing on the back of a receipt.

Another important aspect of the whiteboard methodology is its different approach and attitude to price compared with many other sales methodologies. Let's look at this in more detail now.

Price

A mistake that many new businesses – and some more established ones – make is to lead with price in sales. I was recently working with a financial firm that sells research into listed companies, and their pitches were all about their competitive price. Now, some of the value that is created by this company, through their research, is in the millions of pounds. And they charge tens of thousands for it. Despite this, they often get challenged on their price. My advice was to be confident in the value their product was bringing (potentially millions of pounds) and to avoid customers who could not see that value. A secondary tactic would be to refocus their sales strategy on outlining the value they brought rather than on pricing.

In this way price is no longer apologetically presented with a hope and a prayer that the client will accept. Instead you can proudly say, 'Look, I'm going to deliver all this value, and it's only going to cost this price.' If your differentiating factor is that you have a cheap product, then the client will see it as a cheap product and will want the best possible price. They instinctively perceive it as less valuable. Conversely, if you have a high-quality product and are charging a premium price for it, the client who buys it will feel like they have gotten something special.

Salespeople notoriously feel uncomfortable about presenting a price. But we should remember one important thing: the client wouldn't be talking to you unless they were interested in buying what you have to offer. They wouldn't even be investing their time in the meeting. And so it's a two-way street: the client should feel like they're getting a good deal, and you should feel like you're valuing your product or service. With the whiteboard methodology we aim to have our salespeople focused on value first, to feel confident in the fact that their solution is tailored to the client, and to be able to present the price proudly as a result.

With services you're selling a highly skilled person, or a highly skilled set of processes. It is really important not to undervalue what you are bringing to the table. And though, clearly you have to pitch it to the right market and at the correct market pricing, we should also remember that there's nothing wrong with being the most expensive player on the field if you have the services to back that up. The whiteboard methodology helps the client to really get to the heart of what they are trying to achieve and why, and as a result it helps them to work out exactly how much they are willing to pay for a perfect solution. If they decide that your service is too expensive, it will be in the full knowledge of exactly what value they are going to miss out on. They will understand the consequences for their business and for themselves personally in deciding either to buy or to not buy.

Asking great questions

In order to ensure that your whiteboard is as relevant as possible to the client, and to ensure an appropriate solution is offered, it's important to ask your client the right questions in the right way. So let's now look at asking great questions.

There are two types of question: open and closed. Open questions are used to help establish a really good understanding of the client's needs by 'opening' up the conversation. They start with:

- What
- When
- How
- Where
- Who

and do not only ask for a single simple piece of information. For example: 'What is it about this Goal that is important to you?' 'What is the most important business project that must succeed this year?'

Although 'why' is an open question as well it must be used with care. It can come across as aggressive and if used incorrectly can result in the client becoming defensive. For example: 'Why haven't you achieved that goal yet?' 'Why is that important to you?' 'Why do you not have the right skills?' Why questions should never be used as the first or even the second question, and if they are used they need to be managed carefully.

Closed questions are used to clarify and to close down a line of questioning. They give the client an either / or, yes / no, or this / that option. For example, 'Do you want that in red or green?' 'Do you want us to start next week or the week after?' Closed questions should be used to seek clarification, to confirm understanding and to close a part of or a whole conversation.

Think of it like a funnel. You are asking lots of enquiring open questions at the top pf the funnel, more clarifying open questions as you go down the funnel and then closing questions to clarify, summarise and move on.

General open questions
Specific open questions
Closed questions

For example:

Q: Open: What are you most important business outcomes for you and your team this year ?

A: We are tasked with increasing the availability of the service, driving out costs and managing new business projects that come along

Q: Open: What outcome will deliver you the most business benefit?

A: Increasing the availability of our service.

Q: Open: What sort of improvement would you want to see in availability?

A: Reduce unplanned outages by at least 50% by the end of this year.

Q: Closed: So if we could help you reduce your outages by 50% this year that would be a great outcome for you?

A: Yes

Q: Closed: Would you like me to share with you how we can do that for you?

A: Yes

This is an example. You may want to drill down a little deeper and ask a couple more open questions before closing down.

A few things to watch out for with questioning

Take Care 1

When asking open questions the temptation is to ask one and then leap to a closed question. For example:

Q: What is important about this goal? (Open question)

A: It is critical to the business this year.

Q: OK, so this is your most important goal? (Closed question)

In this example asking another open question would help to uncover more information, as follows:

Q: What is important about this goal? (Open question)

A: It is critical to the business this year.

Q: In what way will it be critical to the business? [Or] How is it critical to the business? [Or] How does achieving this goal impact you personally? (All open questions)

You could ask two or three of these open questions before asking a closing question.

Take Care 2

It is also important when asking an open question that it actually is open. For example, this question appears open at first, but then the questioner gives the client two options:

Q: 'What is it about the skills of your team that you need to develop? Is it storage or open systems?'

This closes it down and demonstrates poor questioning skills.

Take Care 3

Listen to the answer. When you ask a question don't immediately begin thinking about the next question. Listen to the client's answer, and only then think about your next question.

Take Care 4

Finally when you ask a question, open or closed, stop talking and let the client think of an answer. It is fine to have long pauses while they think, that is the way the brain works.

Good questions to ask at each stage of the process

1. What are you focused on achieving? **[Goal]**
    a. What is your main goal for this year? The most important thing you need to achieve?
    b. What does success look like for the business and for your personally?

2. What is it about that goal that is important to you? **[Drivers]**
    a. What is it about that goal the drives you personally?
    b. What would achieving that goal mean to your department / team?
    c. What would achieving that goal mean to the business?
    d. What sort of business benefit would you expect from achieving that goal?
    e. What else is important to you about achieving this goal?
    f. What would it mean if you did not achieve that goal?
    g. What knock on benefit could there be in other areas of the business or team if you achieved this goal?

3. What is stopping you from achieving your goal today? **[Challenges]**
   a. What limits you from getting there today?
   b. What have you tried and what was the result?
   c. How would you rate the skills of your team to achieve your goal?
   d. Do you have the right people or enough people to help you achieve your goal? (closed question).
   e. What other areas of the business are not supporting you to achieve your goal?

4. What have you tried already? **[Bridging to the Solution]**
   a. What have you tried already to help you achieve your goal?
   b. What success have you had from your actions to date?
   c. What have you learned from the actions you have taken to date?
   d. What services do we provide for you today that support you achieving your goal?
   e. From what you know about our services how do you feel we could support you?
   f. What thoughts have you had on how to get to your goal?

5. Who do you know that is achieving this goal today? **[Case study]**
   a. Which peers or similar companies do you know who are achieving your goal?
   b. Are there any examples in other areas of the business that may help you achieve your goal?

Using these questions and skills throughout the whiteboard process will greatly help you to connect with your client and to understand their needs.

Not just for sales

Although the whiteboard methodology was principally designed for sales (and we'll explore the different ways it can be used in sales in Chapter 6), it has many other uses as well.

It creates a great questioning structure that can be used for all different kinds of goals. I was using this just the other day as a coaching tool: everyone in the room was helping each other to work out goals for themselves and how to achieve them, using the whiteboard questioning structure.

It works so well in sales because it gets to the heart of emotional motivation and decision making on a personal level. And it is these characteristics that also make it great as a personal tool. It discovers what is important, what someone values, and what benefits could be gained from taking certain actions towards reaching a goal.

In business it can be used for strategizing: working out what your goals should be, prioritising them by looking at why they are important, followed by looking at what is stopping you from achieving them today, seeing if anyone else is already doing it and how that might help, and finally building a strategic plan using all this information to move the business forward.

I know of parents who have used the tool to help their children decide which university to go to. Or another example, which was with a guy I met in a sales training session, we got talking about goals for 2018 and so I brought up the whiteboard technique, and we went through it together. As a result he worked out that in 2018 he wanted to get himself a long term girlfriend. We went through understanding his drivers to achieve this goal, why he was finding this difficult today, and helped him come to the conclusion that there were several actions he could take as part of a solution to reach that goal (for example updating his Tinder profile, getting better photos, going to the gym more etc.). And I remember thinking, 'Wow, this tool really can be used for almost anything!'

Conclusion

The whiteboard methodology is a powerful and versatile tool. Whether it is in the board room of a global corporation helping them decide how to develop their services strategy, with one of your children helping chose a university, or deciding on a strategy for a long term relationship, the Whiteboard methodology can be employed. Because at the heart it is a decision making tool that gets to the root of the motivations.

In sales, building up the Value with a client before discussing your Price is key to a consultative sales approach and the Whiteboard methodology gives you the framework to do this.

Now, before we dive into the next chapter and the structure of the whiteboard, note that at the end of every chapter is one of these 'key takeaways' boxes.

These are for you to make notes on what we've covered while the chapter is still fresh in your memory. So please make use of them!

My key takeaways from the chapter

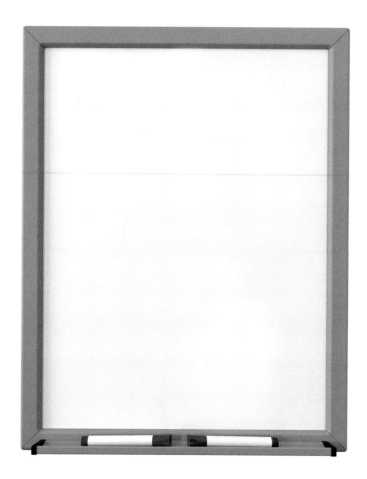

1: BASIC STRUCTURE OF A WHITEBOARD

"Price is what you pay, value is what you get" -
Warren Buffett

As we discussed, the whiteboard has been designed to enable you to have a conversation with your clients and unlock the things that are really important to them and their business, and to demonstrate the value that you can deliver in the services you're selling. Let's look at the basic structure now.

The whiteboard has been designed very simply. It starts with the goal at the centre. The goal is what is important to your client: it's what they're trying to achieve. We put it at the centre so that it's at the heart of the whole whiteboard, the central focus in the middle of all the action. And like all the elements of the whiteboard this has a specific colour for a specific purpose: in this case the goal is written in blue as a strong positive colour.

The goal is supported by the so-called 'drivers'. The drivers are the reason why the client wants to achieve that goal. These run along the top of the whiteboard as the foundation for the client's motivation. What are the most important things for achieving that goal? Why do they want to get there? What's driving them to try to achieve that goal? These are written in black as a solid, foundational colour.

Down the left hand side of the whiteboard are the challenges. What's stopping them from getting there today? Why are they not achieving that goal at the moment? What are the sticking points? These are the issues that, once solved, will help the client to achieve their goal. These are written in red, which in business almost always means something negative, something to be avoided and to move away from.

Over on the right hand side of the whiteboard are the solutions: how you are going to help the client develop a solution to deliver on their drivers so that they can achieve their goal. The solutions section is where you start describing what you do, and how you can add value to their company and what they are trying to achieve. The solutions are written in green: again, this almost universally is a positive signal, meaning 'this will work', 'aim for this'.

Supporting that, around the goal we write the elements that build up the solution you are selling which are called the 'success factors'. These are the different aspects of what you bring to the table to actually achieve the client's goal. And in between these success factors are written clients stories / case studies / evidence to support your claim that the solution will work. Again, these are written in blue as a positive colour.

Conclusion

This, then, is the fundamental structure of the whiteboard. One other important thing to note is that the whiteboard not only uses specific colours in its structure to convey meaning. It's arranged with the challenges on the left and solutions on the right because, in most parts of the northern hemisphere, we read from left to right: our eyes move from the left hand side of the whiteboard to the right. And, importantly, we tend to remember what is written on the right of the Whiteboard or the right of the page - in this case the positive solution section. This is what you want your client to remember when they leave the meeting; what you can bring to the table as a solution. The structure of the whiteboard, then, takes the client on a journey from challenges to solutions.

My key takeaways from the chapter

2: GOALS AND DRIVERS

"What keeps me going is goals" – Muhammad Ali

So, at the centre of the whiteboard is the goal. For TSS we call this Optimised Support: the client's goal in our business is generally to optimise their support structure – what they get from their suppliers, vendors and staff. But the goal can be called whatever you like.

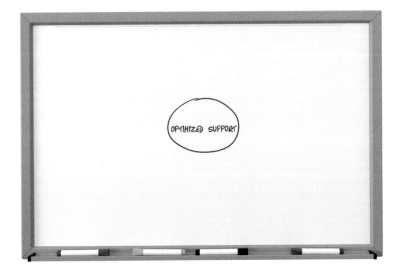

Optimised support is generally driven by four drivers, which are pretty much consistent across most IT organisations. These are availability, cost, efficiency and flexibility. Let's look at these now.

Availability

Availability is key to any IT manager: availability of service, availability to the end user. You won't find anyone in the IT industry who isn't measured on availability at some level, so this is number one on the list.

Cost

Then comes cost: this is critical in the modern world. Again, there isn't any IT department that isn't budget challenged every single year. Cost is key, and we should remember that cost is not just what they're spending on your contract, but about the overall spend of the IT department.

Efficiency

The third driver is efficiency: trying to get the most out of the resources you have, and being efficient in the way you use your resources, the way that you use your team, and in the way you use your capital.

Flexibility

The final driver is flexibility. How can you get the most out of the environment you've got? You've got to be reactive and flexible with new demands that arise. In the twenty-first century situations can change rapidly and departments must be flexible enough to adapt quickly.

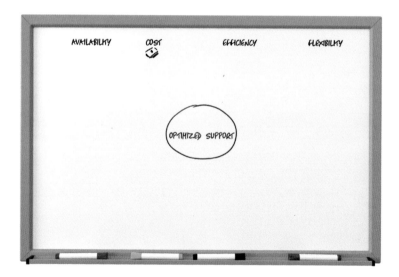

Conclusion

The Goal at the centre of the TSS Whiteboard is Optimised Support, this is a generic and common goal that is a great starting point for the conversations. It would also be difficult to find IT managers that don't have these four drivers within their IT department, and while you can certainly come up with other drivers, if you use those as a conversation start point you're very likely going to be able to open up the conversation easily with your client.

My key takeaways from the chapter

3: CHALLENGES

"Accept challenges so that you may feel the exhilaration of victory" – George S Patton

Let's now look at the challenges part of the whiteboard. Remember that we've got the goal, 'optimised support', in the middle and the drivers written across the top.

A great opening question to ask a client is "what's stopping them from achieving their goals today.? There are typically three answers to this question – three challenges they face that we will usually include on the whiteboard. These are training and skills, service level definitions, and complexity.

Training and skills:
Having the right level of training for their people, and the right skills in the team, to manage all the incoming demands.

Service level definitions:
What are the demands on their business? There are often many different possible demands and therefore many different requirements around service levels that they have to provide to their end user.

Complexity:
IT managers and directors have to manage an incredibly complex environment these days, and this in itself can be a serious challenge.

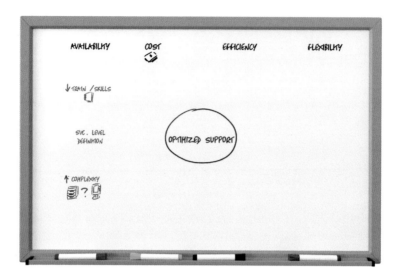

Conclusion

So, these are the three key challenges we almost always build into the whiteboard. Remember, these challenges are written in red and are on the left hand side, because it's where we want to move away from. In the next chapter let's look at where we're moving to.

My key takeaways from the chapter

4: SOLUTION AND SUCCESS FACTORS

"Identify your challenges, but give your power and energy to solutions" – Anthony Robbins

With the solution and success factors sections we are now introducing our service to the client. We'll show them what we can offer, how it will transform their business, and the different elements of what we offer that will deliver that success. So, to address the challenges we introduce the structure of the solution section, from reactive (1) to proactive (2) up the value (3) chain in blue on the right.

Solution

On the right of the whiteboard we start to build up the value that we will deliver to the client and how our services will support this. The TSS solution is to take the client on a journey from Reactive support to one of Proactive support, allowing real value to be delivered to the client as we progress. The solution is built up in Green.

Break-Fix

On the whiteboard we'll start this journey at the bottom of the right-hand side with break-fix: someone has a problem, they log a call and an engineer turns up to solve the issue.

Integrated Software and Hardware Support

The next step up from here – above break-fix on the whiteboard – is integrated software and hardware support. This means integrating all the non-IBM hardware and software with all the IBM hardware and software, bundled into one contract.

Proactive Managed Services

The final step up, which signifies the highest level of value in the solution section's journey towards their goal, is proactive managed services. This means that we're looking at the client's working environment, and we're helping them understand how they can increase their availability,

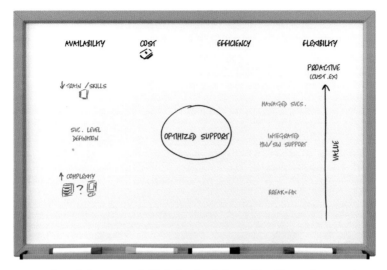

reduce their costs, and think ahead to help avoid ending up in a reactive situation. Obviously this will vary slightly depending on the client, and much more detail can be included on what exactly can be done, but this is the universal framework.

Success factors

The success factors on the whiteboard are the tools that enable us – the company selling the service – to delivery on the promised solution in order to help the client achieve their goal. In IBM TSS these success factors are people, process, and technology:

People:
This means the right people with the right skills in the right place at the right time.

Process:
IBM's decades of experience means that they have tried and tested rock-solid processes in place to see improvements in all of the drivers.

Technology:
This means utilising the best and latest technology in the industry to support clients.

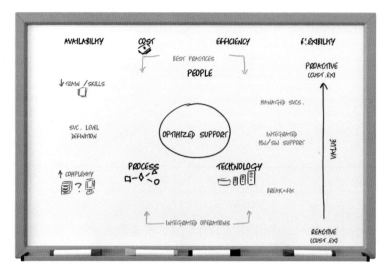

Overarching this are the best practises which enable IBM to keep learning, developing and improving, building on decades of experience. And then underpinning all of these elements are the integrated operations, which link it all together.

Conclusion

This journey we're taking the client on is a conversation we have that helps them understand how we can address their business needs. We need to spend plenty of time talking about their drivers and their challenges to make sure that we don't just leap into a solution, and where we can add value from reactive to proactive having built up that understanding of their environment first, and where we have a dialogue on the success factors with relevance to their particular situation.

My key takeaways from the chapter

5: CASE STUDIES

"Next to doing the right thing, the most important thing is letting people know you are doing the right thing" – John D Rockefeller

The final secret ingredient in the whiteboard selling method is your selection of case studies: client examples of when you or your company have already helped clients achieve their goal of optimised support. The picture is not complete until you've given a really good client story that explains how you helped someone in the past with a very similar situation to the current client. Speaking theoretically alone is greyscale – stories add colour.

This makes them feel like they're not the first. It makes them feel like their problems are not unique. It helps them understand that you know what you're doing and gives them confidence in you. A client story is the absolutely essential icing on the cake. I cannot stress enough that telling a relevant story when you're building the whiteboard will help you in your conversations with the client, and will help to secure their business.

What makes a good case study?

A good case study is something the client can relate to that is relevant for their situation and their business. Remember that we covered how to ask the right questions to fully understand your client's needs in the Introduction ('Asking great questions' section). Good case studies will be about companies with the following:

- From a similar industry – doesn't have to be the same, but needs to have similarities, i.e. banking and insurance or consumer packaged goods and retail
- With a similar Goal and a similar set of Challenges
- With a positive experience of your services
- A similar size of company
- A company that went on a journey with you, from where they were to where they are now – this ideally would include tangible values that

your services achieved, i.e. they were able to increase availability or reduce outages by x%, saving the company £x.

In addition you should always have two or three client stories or case studies ready in your 'toolkit' that you are able to use at any time. When you are using a case study it is best not to use the actually name of the company, but a description that makes it clear the type of company it is, i.e. a medium-sized retail bank in the UK, or a large German car manufacturer.

Ideally you would want to talk about how you were personally involved in helping the company achieve a certain goal, as this helps to bring even more credibility and life to the case study.

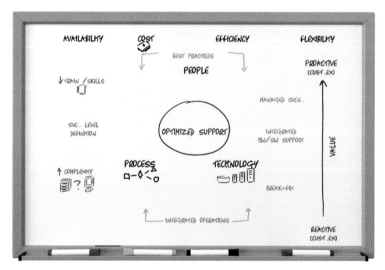

Conclusion

You should now have a solid understanding of why we use case studies and how to go about using them with the whiteboard. They are essential to take everything you are saying out of the theoretical and put it into a real-world situation that the client can relate to and understand. Make sure to ask great questions in order to tailor your case studies to your particular client.

My key takeaways from the chapter

6: EXAMPLES: USES OF THE WHITEBOARD

"The more you focus on the value of your service, the less important price becomes" – Brian Tracy

In the introductory chapter we discussed how the whiteboard could be used in a variety of contexts, not solely for business, and explored those other uses. In this chapter we'll instead look more specifically at the different business contexts where the whiteboard can be useful.

There are four main situations: the first and most obvious is a face-to-face meeting, for which it was designed. An in-person sales meeting where you can write out the whiteboard and build it with the client's input right in front of them is ideal.

The second is on a phone call. Although the client won't be able to see the whiteboard in front of them, nonetheless you can use it to structure your conversation, investigating their drivers and challenges, asking them the right questions, and moving them towards a solution.

A third important use of the whiteboard is when preparing for a sales meeting with a client. You can get everything straight in your head about what they need and how you can tailor the pitch to them, and it will give the meeting a helpful structure.

The fourth situation where the whiteboard can be useful is with a request for purchase (RFP). When a client sends this out they will often have given you the information needed to fill out a lot – but not all – of the whiteboard. You can then look at what is missing and ask them further questions to get all the info you need. Then when you reply to the RFP you will be able to address their needs fully, ensuring that your solution responds to all of their challenges and drivers, and is backed up by case studies. Essentially your response to an RFP is like a written-down version of a whiteboard presentation, which ensures that you cover everything needed.

Conclusion

While the whiteboard was designed for face-to-face sales meetings, it's clear that it is a very useful tool in many different business situations. Essentially it can work as a checklist, ensuring that you have got all the required information from the client, asking all the necessary questions, and have then responded to their situation fully and appropriately in order to present your solution.

My key takeaways from the chapter

7: VALUE

"Price is only ever an issue in the absence of value"
– Anon

In the introduction to this book we briefly covered the difference between logical and emotional value and why it's important to address both of these when dealing with a client. This chapter will focus more narrowly on what exactly we mean by the value of a service in the context of the IT service industry, as well as specifically on how the TSS offerings can address clients' needs and bring them value. We must be sure of this ourselves in order to clearly demonstrate and explain to clients how our services will benefit them.

The three categories of value

In the IT service industry when we are talking about value typically we mean one or more of three different categories:

- Reduced Downtime
- Redeployment of existing resources
- Bringing projects forward

These are the three categories which will relieve pressure from the client's four drivers (availability, cost, efficiency, flexibility) and help them overcome their challenges (training and skills, services level definitions, complexity). Let's look at them now.

Downtime

Downtime is when the client's front end is not available to users. When this is down the client loses out in three key ways.

- First is the actual cost of recovering from a failure, which can be extensive. There's also the cost of keeping people on payroll just in case there's a failure, which can be significant as well.

- Second is the lost business which can result from downtime. If your client has a web front end, and new customers are unable to access it, then they will not wait around for it to come back online. They will simply go to the next best competitor and buy from them. That's business that your client will have lost forever.

- The third, slightly less tangible, aspect is loss of brand value or loss of reputation. If existing customers cannot access the client's services – especially if they are trying to make, for example, an insurance claim, or something else urgent and important – they will make a lot of negative noise about the company. There is also the issue of reputation within the industry: you don't want to be known as the company who constantly has downtime issues.

There are different ways to calculate the total cost of downtime for a particular client, and both you and they can do research to come up with a figure, taking into account these three factors. For most of the companies we deal with, an hour of downtime will cost them over £100,000. We would then multiply that by the number of hours of downtime per year. Just twelve failures a year, one hour per month, could be costing them over a million pounds.

Reduced downtime, then, is clearly going to provide huge monetary benefits

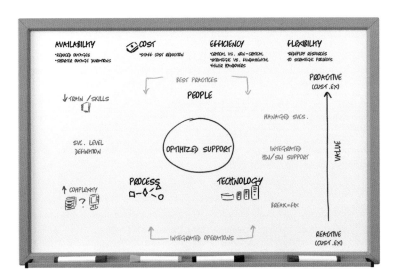

to the client. Being able to assign a value to the cost, and therefore being able to compare this to the relatively minor costs of the TSS offerings, will make it clear to the client just how much value for money they are going to get. With 24/7 world-class support in place reduced downtime is all but guaranteed. And on top of that a lot of our services are automated, and we have skills in-house: the cost for us to deliver them is therefore significantly lower than it would be for the client to do so for themselves.

Redeploying or not replacing staff

As well as the direct cost-saving value of the service, there will also be follow-on value: maybe now that IBM has taken on some of the tasks that the department used to do there will be staff and IT resources freed up. This doesn't necessarily mean a difficult conversation about firing people. Perhaps we can redeploy them. Or perhaps they are people that would have left anyway, and we can simply not replace them.

If we reduce the IT team size in this manner then the cost saving per year of no longer employing those staff members – including pensions, national insurance, salary and benefits – can be significant. Perhaps £100,000 per person, depending on speciality. This is the first aspect of follow-on value.

Bringing projects forward

The second aspect of follow-on value is that those staff who we have freed up for redeployment typically know the organisation and know the systems. This means that typically they can be put to work on other important things.

At any one time, most IT departments will have a number of projects running. These projects aren't running simply because the team want to run them. They're running because they're delivering real value to the client. And often, projects fall behind on schedule. So what if we redeployed some of those freed-up staff to work on the projects?

Generally the value of bringing a project forward by just a few days or a month is significant. The additional manpower can get things back on track, or perhaps deliver additional benefits that weren't expected in the original business case. For example, say the client had a project that was going to deliver a million pounds a month of additional revenue through the deployment of an application, but it was running behind by a month. If they could redeploy some staff that were no longer needed in their old roles to this project and get it back on schedule, that would bring the client one million pounds. The arithmetic really speaks for itself.

Value and the TSS offerings

So, how exactly do the TSS offerings help in delivering this value? Remember that, using the whiteboard, we are taking them on a journey that begins with reactive services, where clients are feeling pressure from their drivers (availability, cost, efficiency, flexibility) and having difficulties with their challenges (training and skills, services level definitions, complexity). The next steps are then hardware maintenance, integrated software and hardware support, and finally proactive managed services. Let's look at how these next three steps add value for the client (for a full list of TSS offerings see the Appendix at the back of the book).

Hardware maintenance

With basic hardware maintenance IBM ensures that hardware is properly maintained. How does this deliver value to the client?

In terms of availability it reduces outages and length of outages: it helps to prevent things going wrong and, if they do, they are fixed more quickly. In terms of costs these are reduced because the client's staff will not be working on a Saturday night to maintain hardware being paid overtime; this also helps with flexibility as the workforce will be available when they are needed, not taking time off in lieu after a weekend of work. And a better hardware maintenance service will also mean a more efficient operating environment in general.

Hardware maintenance may not help too much with training and skills or with complexity, but it will absolutely help with service level definitions: IBM can assist the IT department in defining and developing business strategies they need in order to deliver.

Integrated hardware and software services

Integrated hardware and software services with IBM is the second level of offering we provide. It means hardware maintenance, software maintenance and multi-vendor services. Pulling all this together under one agreement adds value to the client in the following ways.

In terms of availability, outages are reduced because there are fewer handoffs between suppliers and there are no arguments between suppliers over who should be carrying out the maintenance. There is only one service contract supported by one supplier, so the service standard will be the same across all your client's products, and it is clear whose responsibility the maintenance is (IBM's). Having this same consistent standard across the entire estate will also improve efficiency in the environment and service level definitions.

With costs the client makes savings both externally and internally. Externally, by pulling all the contracts together into one a better price is almost guaranteed compared to having individual contracts with different suppliers. And internally there will be no need to negotiate new contracts with new suppliers, which each would have a significant cost: management time, legal time, procurement time. All of that is no longer necessary. Additionally the client's team would no longer have to spend time (and therefore money) managing any conflict and handoffs with suppliers.

IBM takes all of this on for them, and so the team has more flexibility in what they are doing with their time. They are able to focus on higher value things such as training and skills or project work, and not worry about the operational issues at data centre level.

Finally, complexity is greatly reduced. Only having to manage one contract rather than a potentially large number makes things much simpler, reducing the day to day complexity of dealing with multiple suppliers.

Proactive support

The final level of service that the TSS offers is managed services – proactive support. This is the most exciting part of what IBM offers, and is the best conversation that you'll have with the client. It's about looking at the areas that are in need of attention and anticipating things that are going to go wrong before they do. In a similar way to the previous two levels value can be delivered to the drivers and challenges, but in this case that value will be even more significant.

Will it reduce outages? Of course! For example, with Total Microcode Support (TMS), if IBM are managing this in advance and keeping it up to date then this will clearly reduce unwanted outages. Or similarly if a client is using Proactive System Check (PSC) and their storage environment is being managed proactively and problems are being anticipated then again, outages will be reduced.

Costs will be reduced and efficiency and flexibility increased because less of the team's time and resources will be spent on dealing with issues. Additionally in a more available environment the team can be more flexible and can spend more time on higher value projects and tasks – including training and skills. They will also have the service they need to be able to deliver on their own service level definitions to their end users.

Finally, complexity will be greatly reduced because there is just one person to deal with at IBM and they are managing things proactively. They're thinking ahead, they're building a picture proactively of what is needed to increase the availability and reduce the costs of the environment.

Conclusion

So, how does IBM offer value? TSS delivers through preventing outages and the associated costs. Through preventing lost business that occurs during downtime. TSS helps them by reducing the cost of their people or reducing the cost of their operating expenditure. To redeploy scarce skills to other projects that might deliver more value to the business. To move away from the reactive space of managing day to day operations so they can focus on adding more value and on developing the business going forward.

Be sure, as you're having a conversation with a client, to map on the whiteboard against their drivers and challenges all the elements of the proposed solution. Spell out how the solution is helping them to add real value. Because remember, value only counts if it has value in the eyes of the client. Then add a real pound note value to their costs and potential savings, something that's measurable and tangible, something that they can use to compare against the cost of IBM's offerings. This way you will communicate effectively the value of the services you are offering

My key takeaways from the chapter

8: BUILDING VALUE AND PRESENTING YOUR PRICE

"It's not hard to make decisions when you know the value"– Roy Disney

Let's have a look at how this whole process might work in a potential client discussion.

The scenario is that the sales person or business partner rep – Des (D) is meeting with his client's CIO Mark (M).
The client has an IBM hardware and software maintenance contract with you today that costs $1.8M per annum, and $1.0M of hardware and software maintenance on non-IBM equipment. Mark has told Des in an email that he must save 20% on his IBM maintenance contract.
This whole scenario conversation would probably not happen exactly like this over one meeting, but it gives you an idea how the conversation might play out.

D: Hi Mark!

M: Hi Des, good to see you!

D: I know you don't have long and I know that you wanted to talk about your services support you have with IBM today.

M: Yes, I really need to focus on how we can optimise our support, and reduce the IBM maintenance contract by 20%.

D: So your goal is Optimised Support – do you mind if I stand up and put that on the whiteboard to help build a picture of our conversation?

M: No – that would be great.

D: (Draws a circle with Optimised Support in the centre) – Des, please could you share with me your main Drivers for wanting to achieve Optimised Support?

M: Sure – the two main Drivers I can think of are increasing system Availability and reducing Costs.

D: (Writes these on the top of the whiteboard) – That's great thanks –

How many outages do you have today and what would you like to reduce it to?

M: We have 10 hours per annum and I would like to reduce it to 5 hours maximum.

D: (Draws 10 down to 5 on the whiteboard under Availability) Do you know the cost an hour of outage costs you today?

M: Yes it costs about $100k per hour of lost business.

D: (Adds $500k saving under availability) Do you mind if I ask how much you need to reduce your costs by?

M: I need to take out roughly 20% of my external spend – so $200k and reduce my headcount by two.

D: (Add $200k saving below Cost and two heads below Cost) – What does a head cost you today?

M: Roughly $100k per head.

D: (Adds $200k saving below Cost on the whiteboard) typically we are finding that our clients also have business Drivers around Efficiency of their operations and Flexibility of their staff and infrastructure, would you say these were also Drivers for you ?

M: Yes I would......................

The building up of the Whiteboard continues with the questioning and then digging deeper to get some qualitive value.

Presenting your pricing.

So you have now built up a picture of the benefits the client is hoping to see. Let's list these.

- Reduce outages by 50% saving $500k of lost business
- Reduce external spend by $200k
- Reduce headcount by 2 people a saving of $200k
- Start a critical project a month early delivering $500k of business benefit

A total benefit to the client of $1.4M

Your Solution to the client is the following

- Implement committed recovery services (CRS) to reduce outage by 3 hours ($300k saving)
- Add all other manufactuerer maintenance contracts (MVS) to the IBM contracts for 60% of the external spend – giving a $400k saving on current spend and reduce outage time due to working with one supplier reduce outages by 2 hours ($200k saving)
- Implement the full set of proactive services (TMS, PSC and ETS) which will help reduce headcount by 2 heads ($200k) or 1 head and release 1 head to focus on the new web based project – deliver this project 1 month early which is $500k benefit

Client Value:

Reduced outage hours - $500k
Reduce external spend - $400k
Reduce headcount - $100k
Deliver project early - $500k
Total Value - $1.6M.

Imagine that this value benefit goes on the left hand side of a set of balance scales.

VALUE   PRICE

VALUE
$1.6M

PRICE
$0.93M

Now let's look at the pricing.

IBM Maintenance contract today $1.8M, Non IBM Maintenance $1.0M –
Total Spend Today $2.8M.

You are selling the following products:

- Existing IBM maintenance contract – price $1.8M
- Committed Recovery Services – price $180k
- Non IBM Maintenance – price $600k (40% saving on todays price)
- Proactive Services – Total Microcode Support (TMS), Enhance
  Technichal Support (ETS), Proactive System Check (PSC) – combined
  price $150k
- Total new IBM maintenance contract price $2.73M

The difference between the old IBM Maintenance contract price and the
new one is an increase of $0.93M, if we put this on the right hand side of the
balance scales.

So for an additional spend with IBM of $0.93M the client will save $1.6M and net benefit of $0.67M, a 24% saving.

Back to Des and Mark

Des: So Mark are you happy with this solution that we have built for you using all the IBM services and the value you are receiving as a result?

Mark: Yes I am delighted. Your Whiteboard methodology has helped open up new ways of thinking for me and helped me understand the value that your services can deliver for our business.

Des: Please could I ask you to sign the contract so we can get started on delivering this value.

Mark: Yes very happy to............. Thank you.

9: CONCLUDING THOUGHTS

"Knowledge is of no value unless you put it into practice"– Anton Checkov

There was once a priest in a church who did a sermon on a Sunday. It was great and the congregation loved it, leaving with much to think about. Then the next Sunday they came back and he did the same sermon again. They were slightly confused, wondering whether the priest had forgotten that he'd already done it. But on the third week when they returned he did it again. Nobody was sure whether to say anything. On the fourth week, and the fourth repetition of the sermon, the church warden decided to have a word with the priest. 'Do you realise that you've done the same sermon every Sunday for the past four weeks? he asked. And the priest replied, 'Of course and I will keep doing it until you starting doing what I preach!"

Although we don't want to go to the same extremes as the priest, he does have a point: going over something several times is the way we learn. Repetition is the mother of all skills they say. And so this conclusion section will bring together everything that we've already covered in the book.

Summary of the whiteboard

So let's recap on how the whiteboard works. At the centre is the goal, in blue, which for our clients is optimised support. What contributes to this desire for such a goal? The four drivers – the areas where pressure is being put on their IT department, which go in black across the top – which are: the demand for availability of their service; the cost of running their environment and their resources; the need for greater efficiency; and flexibility in the face of rapid changes in the modern world.

What's stopping them from achieving that today? Their challenges. Appearing in red down the left hand side, signalling that they are something to move away from, toward the solutions on the right. The challenges for almost every client are training and skills, service level definitions, and complexity.

Moving to the right side we have the solutions in green. In this section we take the client on a journey from the bottom of the whiteboard – reactive, break-fix support – to the top of the board, through integrated hardware and software support up to proactive, managed services. We're demonstrating the value that we can add to get them there.

To complete the picture we have the success factors (how we're actually going to help them) of people, process and technology, interspersed with case studies and client stories showing how you've done this before. Finally this central part of the whiteboard is visually encased by best practices and integrated operations.

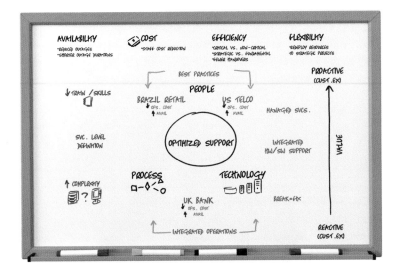

Underlying all of this is the key idea that the value of your product must be relevant to the client: the whiteboard links their needs to your offerings.

Where to go from here

Having read this quick guide you have a very simple, effective, proven structure for having conversations with clients, for engaging with people at all levels in a company, and for helping manage a thought process which directs them towards your solution to address their issues.

As with learning anything new, unless you use it, try it, take some risks, be courageous and simply get out there and do it you will quickly forget what you've learned and will not improve.

So go try it! First you can try it out in a safe environment, such as with your colleagues or family. And then go and try it in front of a client, but ask their permission first so that they know you are planning to talk to them in a particular, structured way.

Whatever you do, don't just read the pages of the book, put it down and do nothing with it. Really think about how this could be useful for you, and when and how you could utilise the whiteboard technique in your day to day lives. Below we have left space for you to write down your thoughts on this while the ideas are still fresh – and we would encourage you to write them down now!

What am I going to do differently and by when?
How will I use in my day to day work?

APPENDIX: SUMMARY OF THE TSS OFFERINGS

Hardware Maintenance

The TSS core hardware support offering after warranty for IBM and non-IBM products.

Software Maintenance

An inseparable combination of support and subscription for software on power and storage systems: the operating systems and operating system related software (licensed program products, e.g. six virtualisation (PowerVM), file systems (GPFS)). the support part entitles a client to open service tickets at IBM to get support. Without a software maintenance contract, a client will not get support and can only raise product defects to IBM in relation to the software license agreement. In that case IBM will decide when to analyse the problem and when to fix the issue. The subscription part allows the customer to access SW upgrades and updates to keep the system up to date and protected.

Enhanced Technical Services

A complimentary service for all hardware platforms, providing additional enhancements compared to the prerequisite base services (Warranty, Hardware Maintenance, Software Maintenance, Support Line) and proactive advice and information to avoid problems.

Total Microcode Support

Provides a proactive service, where IBM will analyse all contracted systems in relation to the installed microcode. The client will be presented, in a meeting with a report, with all information about the eight installed microcode levels and the recommended microcode level to be installed on each system. Optionally IBM or the business partner can offer and perform the installation of the recommended actions. The analysis and recommendation is performed by IBM Support Specialists with deep technical skill and experience who also consider how the systems are being used and engage IBM dedicated analysis systems to automatically, without any risk of human error, check for common denominators.

Proactive System Check for Storage

A detailed system check comparable to the regular inspection of a car. It uses a predefined product dependent check list, including all items and conditions to be checked, and provides the findings and results back to the client. As a result the client will know what needs to be done to ensure and protect the product availability. The service was developed on request of the IBM Support Teams, as they were receiving many problems which could have been avoided with such a proactive approach. Storage is a fast growing platform and we recognise that client IT administrators are becoming more and more busy with installing and adding new storage components and maintaining and updating existing systems.

Multi-Vendor Services

Provides maintenance services for non-IBM products and is comparable to Hardware Maintenance for IBM products. Provides Software Support for non IBM Software – the available service scope depends on the vendor. For main platforms such as Microsoft, VMware ESX, Novell SLES, Redhat RHEL etc. collaboration with the vendors is established, enabling a full end-to-end support.

Opensource Software Support

The Opensource Software Support offering provides an enterprise class support option for free open source software products. This offering removes the main inhibitor to the rapid deployment and cost reduction benefits associated with free opensource software adoption. This enables increased availability by providing problem diagnosis, non-defect 'how to' enquiries and access to security fixes to reduce malicious threats to IT services and data.

ABOUT THE AUTHOR

Neil Thubron is a sales and leadership coach, mentor and teacher, and a professional public speaker. He is passionate about sales and selling value.

Neil joined IBM as a typewriter engineer in 1984. At 22 years old he became a manager, one of the youngest in IBM's history. He then moved into sales and found his passion for selling. He continued in sales for the rest of his career, moving into sales management, then as a UK Sales Director of Technology Support Services and finished his career as European Head of Sales Technology Support Services managing 450 sales people in 60 countries across Europe from the east coast of Russia to the west coast of France, From Iceland to Israel. He retired from corporate life at the age of 50 in 2015.

Outside of his work life he joined the British Army Reserves in 1988 and went on to complete some of the toughest challenges set for British soldiers. He was commissioned as an officer through Sandhurst College in 1990. He spent 12 years in the Army Reserve, with the last eight years in the Royal Engineers 101st (EOD) Regiment, a bomb disposal unit.

The army sparked Neil's interest in physical challenges: in 2003 he completed his first marathon, which then led onto other more extreme physical challenges including an Ironman, the Marathon Des Sables in the Sahara desert, the Ultra Trail de Mont Blanc, the Kalahari Augrabies Extreme Marathon in the desert in South Africa and the Yukon Arctic Ultra.

Today Neil is the founder of Extreme Energy – XNRG – Ltd who organise single and multiday ultra distance events in the UK as well as corporate charity cycling events and team building events.

He is also a coach, consultant and teacher that helps companies develop their leadership and sales teams using the whiteboard methodology. He helped IBM develop their TSS academy and he teaches at many of the TSS Academy Champion training events around the world.